A LEARNING WORKS SKILL BUILDER

WHO'S LISTENING?

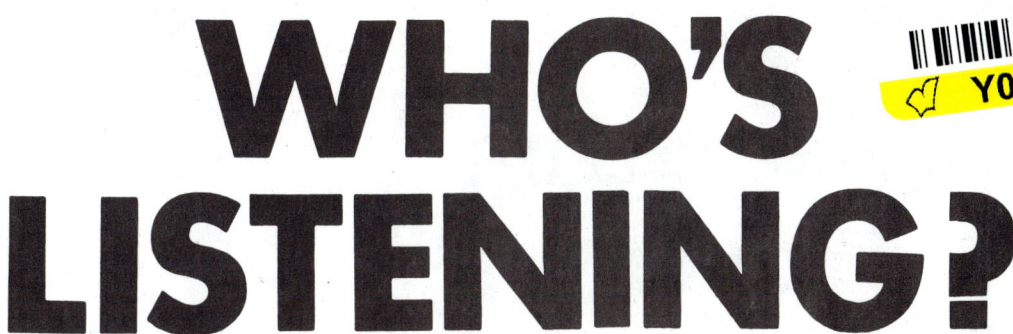

GRADES 1-3

WRITTEN AND ILLUSTRATED BY BEVERLY ARMSTRONG

The Learning Works

THIS BOOK BELONGS

TO

_____

The purchase of this book entitles the individual teacher to reproduce copies for use in the classroom.

Copyright © 1981 - THE LEARNING WORKS, INC.
All rights reserved.
Printed in the United States of America.

Name _____

WATCH THE BIRDIE

Name _____

BIG AND LITTLE CRITTERS

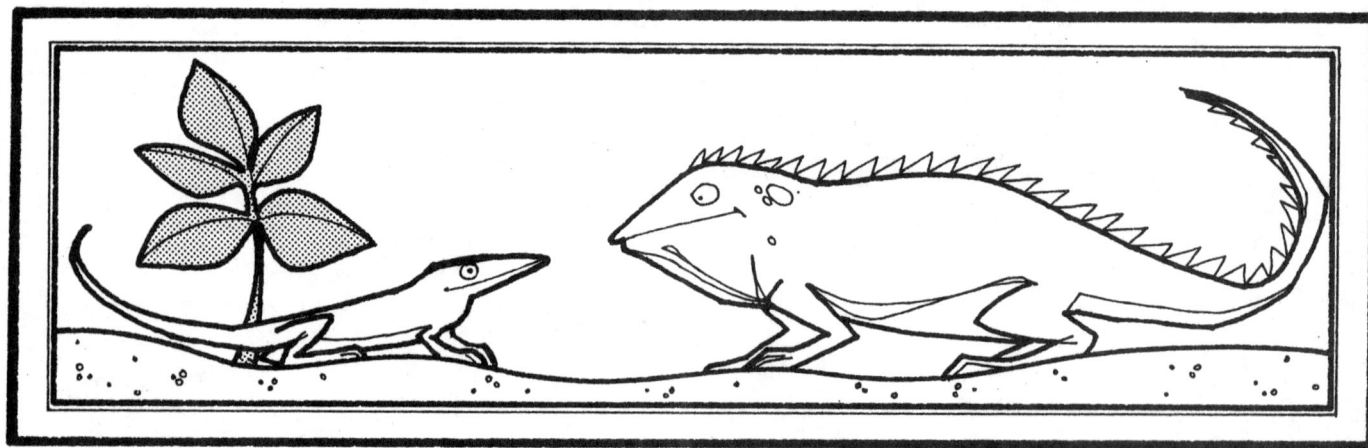

Name _____

MONSTER, MONSTER, MONSTER

WHO'S LISTENING
COPYRIGHT ©1981—THE LEARNING WORKS, INC.

Name _____

THE FIX-IT SHOP

WHO'S LISTENING
COPYRIGHT ©1981—THE LEARNING WORKS, INC.

7

Name _____

WHAT'S WORKING?

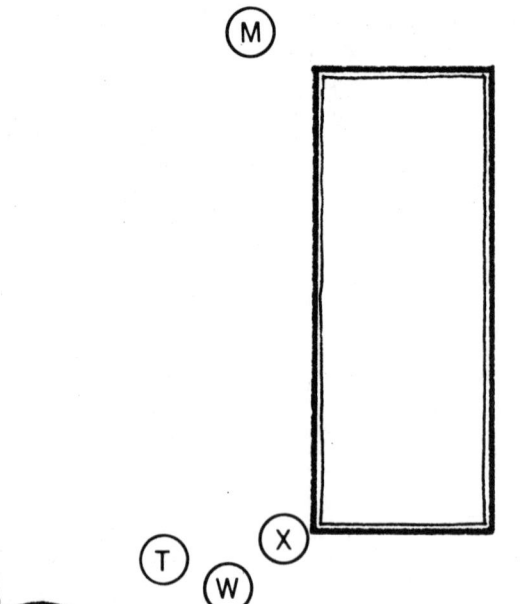

Name _____

WHERE'S THE HORSE?

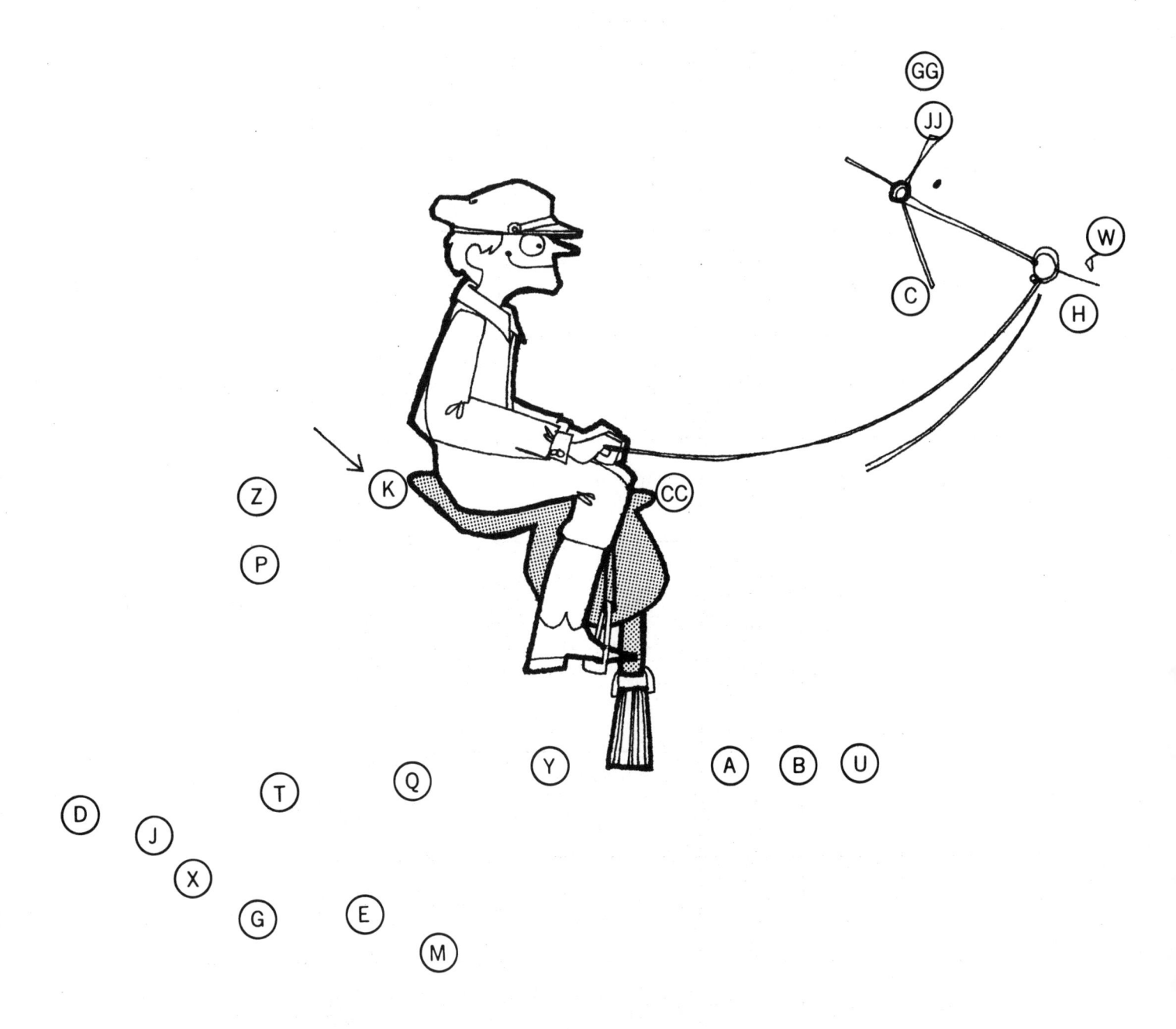

WHO'S LISTENING
COPYRIGHT ©1981—THE LEARNING WORKS, INC.

HIDDEN CRITTER

X	X	X	X	X	F	F	F	F	F
X	X	X	X	X				F	F
X	X	X	X	X		O		M	M
X	X	X	X	X				Q	Q
X	X	X	X	X				Q	Q
X	X	X	X	X				Q	Q
								Q	Q
V								Q	Q
V	V							Q	Q
V	V						Q	Q	Q
Z	Z	Z	G	J	J	J	J	J	J
Z	Z	Z	G	G	G	J	J	J	J

AN AWFUL APPLE

Name _____

SIX FROGS AND A DOG

WHO'S LISTENING
COPYRIGHT ©1981—THE LEARNING WORKS, INC.

12

Name _____

COLORFUL CANDY

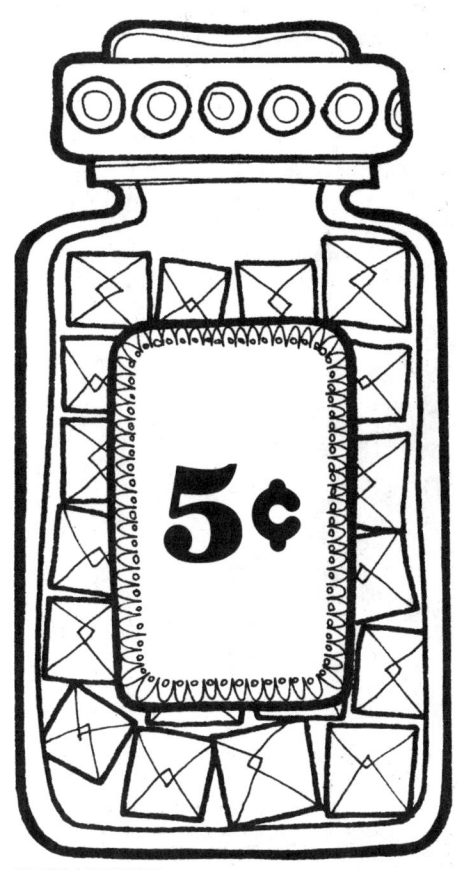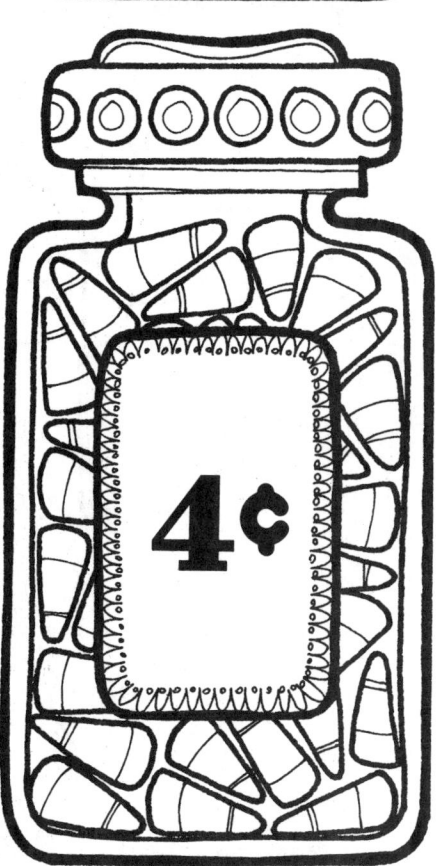

WHO'S LISTENING
COPYRIGHT ©1981—THE LEARNING WORKS, INC.

Name _____

COSTUME CONTEST

14

WHO'S LISTENING
COPYRIGHT ©1981—THE LEARNING WORKS, INC.

Name _____

QUILT SQUARES

15

WHO'S LISTENING
COPYRIGHT ©1981—THE LEARNING WORKS, INC.

Name _____

PICK A PUMPKIN

16

WHO'S LISTENING
COPYRIGHT ©1981—THE LEARNING WORKS, INC.

Name _____

BEARS AND BALLOONS

Name _____

SIX SUPER SNAKES

Name _____

SUPERSCOOPS

Name _____

PENGUIN PARADE

20

WHO'S LISTENING
COPYRIGHT ©1981—THE LEARNING WORKS, INC.

Name _____

FINISH THE PUPPETS

Name _____

PRIZE PETS

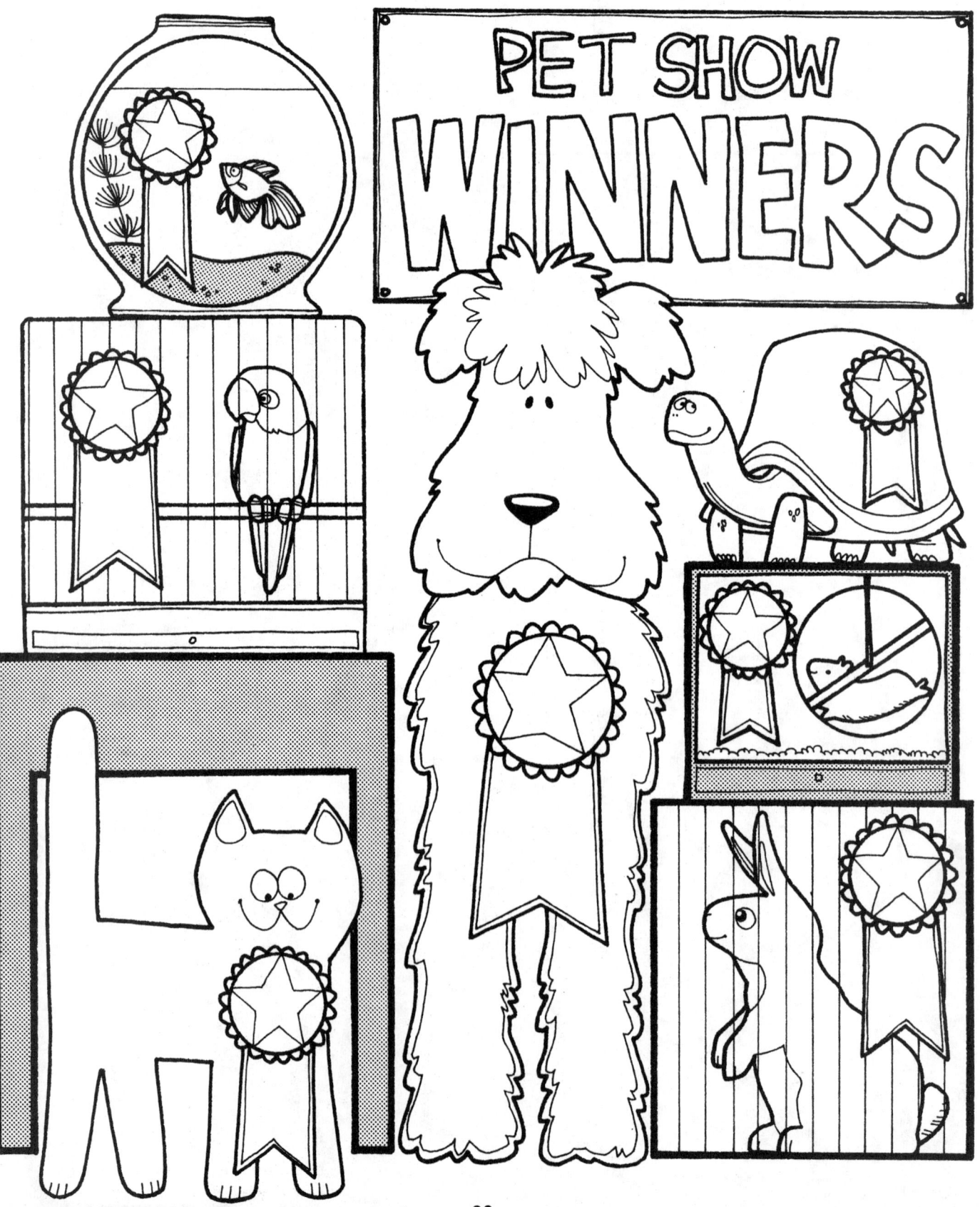

WHO'S LISTENING
COPYRIGHT ©1981—THE LEARNING WORKS, INC.

Name _____

A SPOOKY SPOT

Name _____

FEEDING TIME

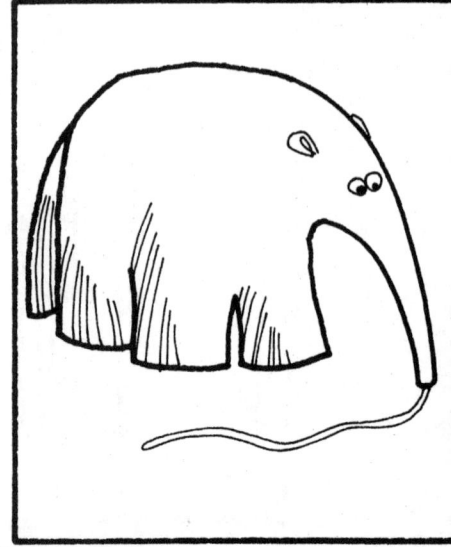

Name _____

MAKE A MARTIAN

WHO'S LISTENING
COPYRIGHT ©1981—THE LEARNING WORKS, INC.

Name _____

ANIMALS IN ACTION

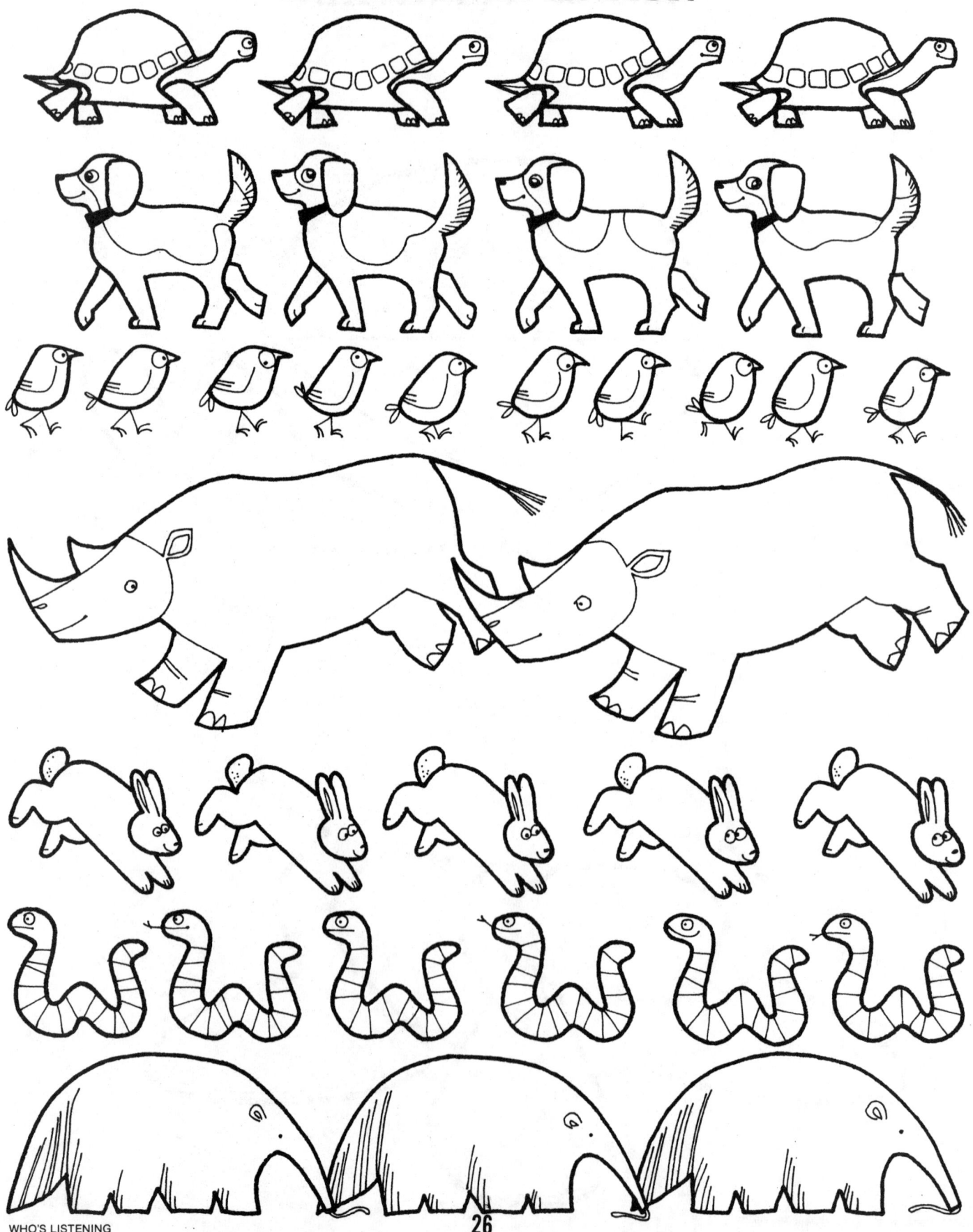

WHO'S LISTENING
COPYRIGHT ©1981—THE LEARNING WORKS, INC.
26

Name _____

LET'S FLY A KITE

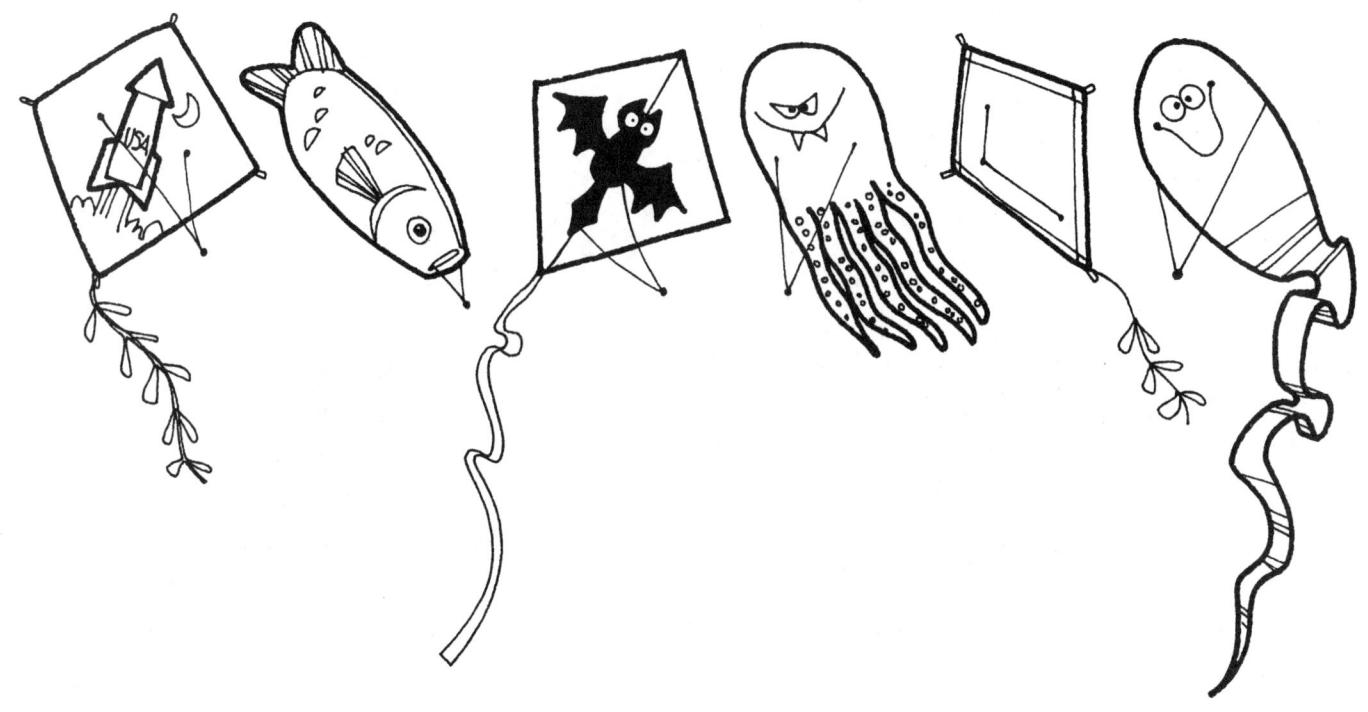

Name _____

CUCKOO CLOCK

Name _____

TRICKY TOYS

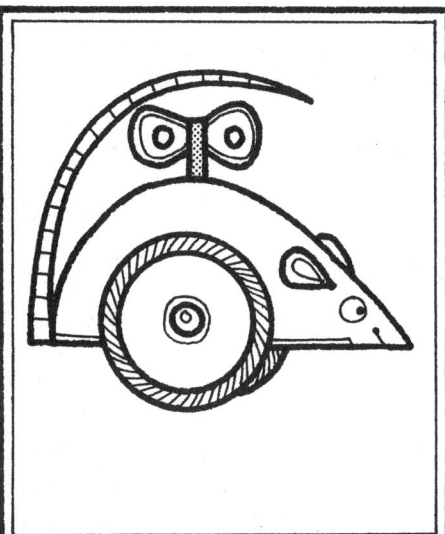

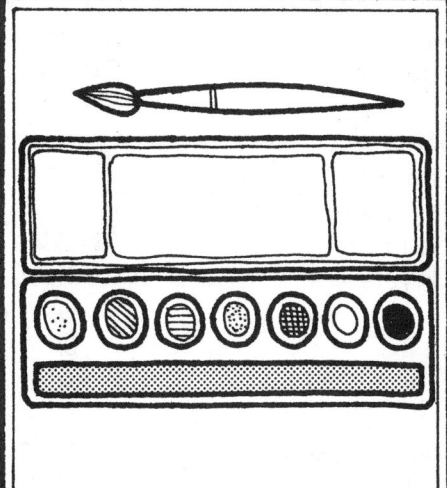

ORAL DIRECTIONS

WATCH THE BIRDIE!—page 3
Color the tallest bird blue.
Color the fattest bird purple.
Color the bird that is sleeping green.
Color the bird with the longest tail red.
Color the bird that is flying orange.
Color the bird with the longest beak yellow.

BIG AND LITTLE CRITTERS—page 4
Color the big fish orange.
Color the little turtle brown.
Color the big bird purple.
Color the big rabbit black.
Color the big lizard green.
Color the little lizard blue.
Color the big turtle yellow.
Color the little rabbit orange.
Color the little bird red.
Color the little fish black.

MONSTER, MONSTER, MONSTER—page 5
Color the middle monster's teeth orange.
Color the left monster's feet green.
Color the right monster's tail purple.
Color the left monster's eyes yellow.
Color the middle monster's horns red.
Color the right monster's ears green.
Color the middle monster's hands purple.
Color the left monster's nose blue.
Color the right monster's neck yellow.

COLOR THE CLOWNS—page 6
Color the left clown's hat purple.
Color the right clown's balloon red.
Color the left clown's suspenders green.
Color the right clown's shoes blue.
Color the right clown's tie yellow.
Color the left clown's pants orange.
Color the right clown's shirt purple.
Color the left clown's shoes green.
Color the left clown's tie red.
Color the right clown's hat orange.

THE FIX-IT SHOP—page 7
Draw another wheel on the skate.
Put hands on the clock.
Make a handle on the shovel.
Draw a cord on the iron.
Put a seat on the bike.
Make a picture on the television screen.
Draw four buttons on the shirt.
Put another wheel on the wagon.
Draw a handle on the suitcase.

WHAT'S WORKING?—page 8
Draw a line from X to Z, then from Z to J.
Draw a line from J to M, then from M to W.
Draw a line from W to R, then from R to D.
Now go from D to Q, then Q to N.
Go from N to T, and T to B.
Go from B to Y, and Y to A.
Go from A to F, then F to L.
Now go from L back to Y.

WHERE'S THE HORSE?—page 9
Draw a line connecting the letters to make a horse for this rider.
Start at K, then go on to the other letters as I name them: Z, D, J, P, T, X, L, S, G, Q, E, O, F, M, Y, A, N, V, B, R, I, U, C, H, W, JJ, GG, CC.

HIDDEN CRITTER—page 10
Color the squares with X in them blue.
Color the squares with J in them green.
Color the squares with M in them yellow.
Color the squares with Q in them blue.
Color the squares with Z in them green.
Color the squares with F in them blue.
Color the squares with G in them yellow.
Color the squares with V in them blue.
Color the square with O in it black.

AN AWFUL APPLE—page 11
Color the worm that is ON the apple blue.
Color the worm going UNDER the apple yellow.
Color the worm BEHIND the apple orange.
Color the worm going THROUGH the apple green.
Color the worm IN FRONT OF the apple brown.
Color the worm going AROUND the top of the apple purple.
Color the worm jumping OVER the apple red.

SIX FROGS AND A DOG—page 12
Put a yellow dot on the frog that is ON the dog.
Put a purple dot on the frog that is BEHIND the dog.
Put a red dot on the frog jumping OVER the dog.
Put a blue dot on the frog running AROUND the dog.
Put an orange dot on the frog that is UNDER the dog.
Put a green dot on the frog that is IN FRONT OF the dog.

WHO'S LISTENING
COPYRIGHT ©1981—THE LEARNING WORKS, INC.

COLORFUL CANDY—page 13
Color the candy that costs 2¢ red.
Color the candy that costs 4¢ yellow.
Color the candy that costs 1¢ green.
Color the candy that costs 3¢ black.
Color the candy that costs 6¢ purple.
Color the candy that costs 5¢ brown.

COSTUME CONTEST—page 14
Put a 1 on the elephant's card.
Put a 2 on the ice cream cone's card.
Put a 3 on the spider's card.
Put a 4 on the penguin's card.
Put a 5 on the cowboy's card.
Put a 6 on the princess's card.
Put a 7 on the witch's card.
Put a 8 on the football player's card.

QUILT SQUARES—page 15
Color two hearts red and one heart purple.
Color one house green and two houses blue.
Color all the butterflies yellow.
Color two stars orange and two stars green.
Color one flower red and two flowers yellow.

PICK A PUMPKIN—page 16
Put a purple X on the pumpkin with two teeth.
Draw a green circle around the pumpkin with four teeth.
Put a red square around the pumpkin with one tooth.
Draw a blue line under the pumpkin with three teeth.
Color the pumpkin with five teeth yellow.
Draw orange ears on the pumpkin with no teeth.

BEARS AND BALLOONS—page 17
Put a purple X on the first bear's balloon.
Color the second bear's balloon yellow.
Make a green face on the third bear's balloon.
Draw red stripes on the fourth bear's balloon.
Make five orange dots on the fifth bear's balloon.
Draw a blue triangle on the sixth bear's balloon.

SIX SUPER SNAKES
Color the first snake red and purple.
Color the third snake blue and green.
Color the sixth snake orange and yellow.
Color the second snake yellow and brown.
Color the fourth snake red and green.
Color the fifth snake purple and blue.

SUPERSCOOPS—page 19
On the first cone, color the top scoop brown and the bottom scoop orange.
On the second cone, color the bottom scoop purple and the top scoop red.
On the third cone, color the top scoop green and the bottom scoop yellow.
On the fourth cone, color the middle scoop red. Color the top scoop orange and the bottom scoop yellow.
On the fifth cone, color the top scoop brown. Color the middle scoop purple and the bottom scoop orange.

PENGUIN PARADE—page 20
Color the flag with the circle red.
Color the flag with the square purple.
Color the flag with the heart yellow.
Color the flag with the triangle blue.
Color the flag with the star green.

FINISH THE PUPPETS—page 21
Draw black ears on the cat.
Put a red hat on the clown.
Give the dog a brown nose.
Make purple hair on the witch.
Give the alligator a lot of green teeth.
Put black eyes on the snowman.

PRIZE PETS—page 22
Color the dog's ribbon red.
Color the turtle's ribbon blue.
Color the cat's ribbon green.
Color the ribbon on the fish bowl yellow.
Color the rabbit's ribbon purple.
Color the hamster's ribbon brown.
Color the ribbon on the bird's cage orange.

A SPOOKY SPOT—page 23
Draw a blue circle around the spider.
Color one bat orange and the other bat black.
Draw a red line under the cat.
Make a purple smile on the ghost at the door.
Color the moon yellow.
Put a green X on the witch.
Color the ghost in the chimney red.

FEEDING TIME—page 24
Draw a purple worm in the bird's beak.
Draw some green grass for the horse to eat.
Give the seal a blue fish.
Draw an orange carrot by the rabbit.
Put some brown leaves on the tree for the giraffe.

WHO'S LISTENING
COPYRIGHT ©1981—THE LEARNING WORKS, INC.

Draw a black fly on the frog's tongue.
Draw some red ants for the anteater.
Give the turtle some green lettuce.
Draw a yellow banana in the monkey's hand.

MAKE A MARTIAN—page 25
Draw orange teeth in the martian's mouth.
Color the martian's eyes yellow.
Make purple claws on the martian's hands.
Give the martian a little green nose.
Draw two blue horns on the martian's head.
Color the martian's feet red.
Make three green spots and three purple spots on the martian's body.

ANIMALS IN ACTION—page 26
Color the first and last turtles green. Color the middle turtles yellow.
Color the two dogs on the left orange. Color the two dogs on the right brown.
Color five birds black and five birds yellow.
Color the rhinoceros on the right red. Color the rhinoceros on the left purple.
Color the first rabbit and the last rabbit black. Color the middle rabbit brown. Color the other two rabbits yellow.
Color the snakes that are sticking out their tongues green. Color the other snakes blue.
Color the middle anteater orange. Color the left anteater red and the right anteater purple.

LET'S FLY A KITE—page 27
Color the first kite blue. Draw a line from this kite to the boy in the striped shirt.
Color the second kite purple. Draw a line from this kite to the girl who is barefoot.
Color the third kite orange. Draw a line from this kite to the boy with the dog.
Color the fourth kite yellow. Draw a line from this kite to the girl with pony tails.
Color the fifth kite red. Draw a line from this kite to the girl who is sitting down.
Color the sixth kite green. Draw a line from this kite to the boy who is pointing up.

CUCKOO CLOCK—page 28
Color the big hand purple and the little hand red.
Color the number between 8 and 10 green.
Put a blue dot on the number to the right of the 7.
Color the 2, the 4, the 8, and the 10 orange.

Draw a red circle around the number that the little hand is pointing to.
Color the bird yellow.
Make a blue line under the number to the right of the 12.
Put yellow squares around the two numbers closest to the 6.
Color the number that the purple hand is pointing to black.

TRICKY TOYS—page 29
Draw a red line under the puzzle and a green line over the puzzle.
Draw a purple circle around the mouse and color the tail red.
Put six brown spots on the horse. Draw a blue triangle above the horse.
Draw a yellow circle around the 5 on the car. Make an orange square around the car.
Make a green X under the paint set. Color the paintbrush purple.
Make a blue dot to the left of the doll. Make a yellow dot to the right of the doll.
Put an orange tail on the kite. Color the stars on the kite yellow.
Make a green square around the dog. Color the dog's ribbon red.
Draw a purple line under the robot. Make a green circle to the left of the robot.

WHO'S LISTENING
COPYRIGHT ©1981—THE LEARNING WORKS, INC.